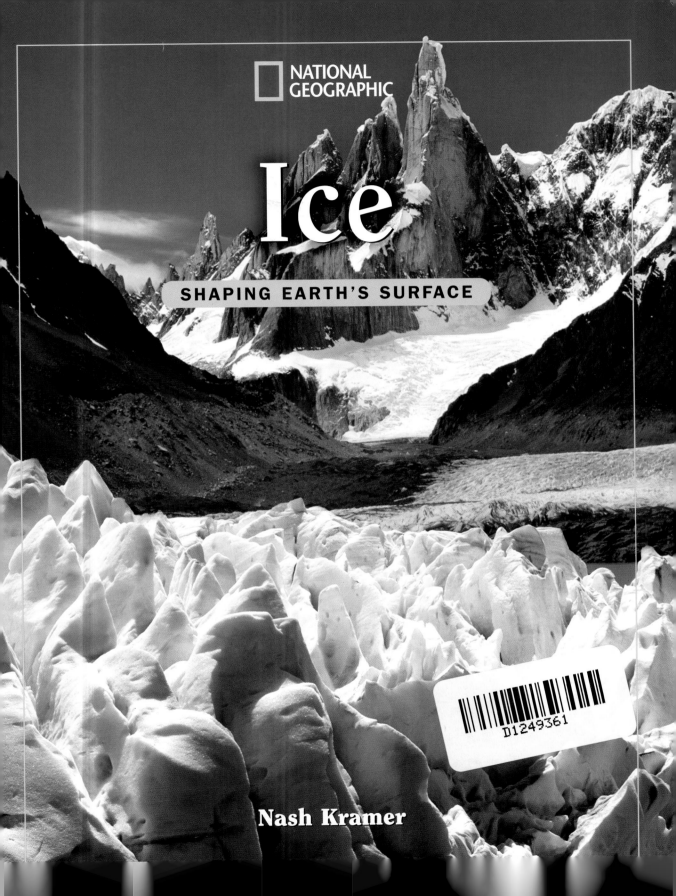

NATIONAL GEOGRAPHIC

Ice

SHAPING EARTH'S SURFACE

Nash Kramer

PICTURE CREDITS

Cover: photograph of glaciers flowing through valleys and mountains © Bill Ross/Corbis/Tranz.

Photographs: page 1, Photodisc; page 4 (bottom left), Corbis; page 4 (bottom right), Photodisc; page 5 (top) © David Muench/Corbis/Tranz; page 5 (bottom left), Photodisc; page 5 (bottom right), Corbis; pages 6-7 © Tom Bean/Corbis/Tranz; page 8 © Stock Image Group/SPL; page 9 © Michael T. Sedam/Corbis/Tranz; page 10 © Richard Hamilton Smith/Corbis/Tranz; page 11 © Tom Bean/Corbis/Tranz; page 12 © Peter Reynolds/Frank Lane Picture Agency/Corbis/Tranz; page 14 © Galen Rowell/Corbis/Tranz; page 15 © Reuters; page 16 © Jonathan Blair/Corbis/Tranz; page 21 © Paul A. Souders/Corbis/Tranz; page 22 © David Muench/Corbis/Tranz; page 24 © NASA/Corbis/Tranz; page 25 (middle left) photograph of drumlin field, northwestern Manitoba, Canada, page 25 (bottom left) photograph of Kettle lakes in Northwest Territory Canada, reproduced with the permission of the Minister of Public Works and Government Services, Canada, 2004 and Courtesy of Natural Resources Canada, Geological Survey of Canada; page 25 (right) photograph of Cape Cod in Massachusetts, United States, courtesy of NASA; page 26 © Andrew Brown Ecoscene/Corbis/Tranz; page 29 © Seth Joel/Taxi/Getty Images.

Illustrations on pages 13 and 19 by Kevin Currie.

Produced through the worldwide resources of the National Geographic Society, John M. Fahey, Jr., President and Chief Executive Officer; Gilbert M. Grosvenor, Chairman of the Board; Nina D. Hoffman, Executive Vice President and President, Books and Education Publishing Group.

PREPARED BY NATIONAL GEOGRAPHIC SCHOOL PUBLISHING
Ericka Markman, Senior Vice President and President, Children's Books and Education Publishing Group; Steve Mico, Vice President and Editorial Director; Marianne Hiland, Executive Editor; Richard Easby, Editorial Manager; Jim Hiscott, Design Manager; Kristin Hanneman, Illustrations Manager; Matt Wascavage, Manager of Publishing Services; Sean Philpotts, Production Manager.

EDITORIAL MANAGEMENT
Morrison BookWorks, LLC

PROGRAM CONSULTANTS
Dr. Shirley V. Dickson, Program Director, Literacy, Education Commission of the States; James A. Shymansky, E. Desmond Lee Professor of Science Education, University of Missouri-St. Louis.

National Geographic Theme Sets program developed by Macmillan Education Australia, Pty Limited.

Published by the National Geographic Society
1145 17th Street, N.W.
Washington, D.C. 20036-4688

ISBN: 0-7922-4748-5

Product 41988

Printed in Hong Kong.

Contents

Shaping
Earth's Surface

Think of all the shapes and forms you can see on Earth's surface. These shapes and forms change all the time. Some changes happen quickly, as when an earthquake or volcano jolts the land. Other changes are slow, as when wind, water, or ice wears away rock. Wind, water, ice, earthquakes, and volcanoes are all forces that shape Earth's surface.

 ## Key Concepts ....

1. Different forces shape the landforms that make up Earth's surface.
2. Earth's surface changes in different ways.
3. People try to control, or at least understand, the effect of forces that shape Earth's surface.

Forces Shaping Earth's Surface

Wind

Wind can change the surface of rock, deserts, plains, and coastlines.

Water

Water can change the landscape by carving out canyons and valleys.

In this book you will learn how ice shapes Earth's surface.

Ice

Ice can slowly change the shape of rock and create new landforms.

Earthquakes and Volcanoes

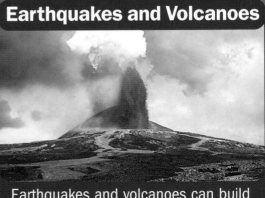

Earthquakes and volcanoes can build landforms and destroy them.

The Effects of Ice

Ice is a powerful force. It can split rocks apart. It can shape landforms such as mountains and valleys. A **glacier** is a large mass of ice that slowly flows over the land. Glaciers change Earth's surface in many ways. These changes happen slowly over thousands of years.

Glaciers exist in cold regions and in high mountains. There are two types of glaciers. One type forms on mountainsides and moves downward through valleys. The second type, called an ice sheet, is much larger. Ice sheets spread out over land. As they slowly flow over the land they alter Earth's features.

Yosemite Valley in California was carved out by a glacier.

Earth's Surface

Earth's surface, or outer layer, is made up of many different types of rocks and soils. These rocks and soils make up **landforms**. Landforms give Earth's surface its shape. Some landforms are mountains, hills, valleys, plateaus, deserts, and plains.

The shape of Earth's surface is changing all the time. Different **forces** cause these changes over time. Some forces cause landforms to be created. Others can cause them to be destroyed completely. Ice, especially in the form of glaciers, is one force that brings many changes to Earth's surface.

landforms
natural shapes on Earth's surface

forces
causes of movement and change

Ice in the form of glaciers shapes landforms such as mountains and plains.

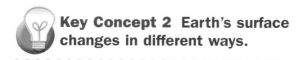

Key Concept 2 Earth's surface
changes in different ways.

How Ice Changes Earth's Surface

Different forces change the landforms on Earth's surface. Two of these forces, **weathering** and **erosion**, are constantly at work. They cause change gradually, over time.

Weathering happens when rock slowly wears away. There are two types of weathering – mechanical and chemical. **Mechanical weathering** happens when something pushes against rock. This causes the rock to break and wear away. One type of mechanical weathering happens when water collects in cracks in rocks. If the temperature drops low enough, the water freezes and expands. As the ice expands, it pushes against the rock, breaking it.

Rocks that have been broken apart by the action of water freezing and thawing

Chemical weathering occurs when rock is dissolved by chemical action. Chemicals in water combine with minerals in rocks. This mixture can dissolve certain types of rock. Warmer temperatures favor chemical action. Because glaciers occur in cold climates, they cause little chemical weathering.

Erosion follows weathering. Erosion is the process in which rock particles, or sediment, are moved from one place to another.

Ice weathering and erosion are caused by the movement of glaciers. Glaciers cause many types of weathering and erosion, most of which occur gradually. As glaciers move they wear away the rocks lying in their path and also those lying beneath them.

Erosion by a glacier shaped this valley through the mountains.

Glaciers and Their Effects

Glaciers are formed when more snow falls in winter than melts in summer. As new snow falls, it covers and packs down the previous layers. The snow builds up until its own weight turns the layers at the bottom to solid ice. Eventually, gravity forces the heavy ice to start moving downhill, like a very slow river. Today, glaciers are found near the North and South Poles and in high mountain valleys.

As a glacier slides over the land, it picks up rock fragments, or debris, along the way. Debris ranges in size from fine sand to huge boulders. As the glacier moves, the debris scrapes the **bedrock**, which is the solid rock under the glacier. Glaciers can carve out basins and scoop out deep valleys in the land.

There are several types of weathering and erosion caused by glaciers.

This rock shows scratches and tiny grooves made by a glacier moving over it.

Plucking One way that glaciers cause weathering and erosion to rock is by plucking. Plucking is the lifting and carrying away of pieces of rock by glaciers. Meltwater underneath a glacier flows into cracks in the bedrock. When the water freezes again it expands. This weakens and loosens the rock, fracturing it. The movement of the glacier then plucks out the fractured rock. This rock material becomes held in the ice and is carried away.

Abrasion The build-up of loose rock, sand, and silt at the bottom of a glacier can rub against bedrock as the glacier moves. This rubbing action is called **abrasion**. The rocks and other sediment in the glacier act like sandpaper rubbing away at a piece of wood. The movement slowly wears away the bedrock. The worn material is then carried along with the glacier.

The brown streaks seen in this glacier in Alaska are deposits of worn material that has been carried along in the ice.

Deposition When a glacier melts or retreats, the load of soil and rock that has been picked up and carried is eventually deposited elsewhere. This process, called **deposition**, changes the shape of landforms.

Eskers are long, narrow ridges of sand and gravel that have been deposited by streams of meltwater flowing beneath a glacier. Eskers may be several miles long. They run downhill in the direction the glacier ice flowed.

Moraines are long, hilly ridges at the edges of a glacier. These landforms are made of material that varies from fine sediment to large boulders. Melting ice deposits this material at the sides and front of a glacier.

Outwashes are wide, flat plains made of sand and gravel. They form when large amounts of meltwater wash out sand and gravel from the moraine.

Glacial outwash in Iceland

Diagram of a Glacier

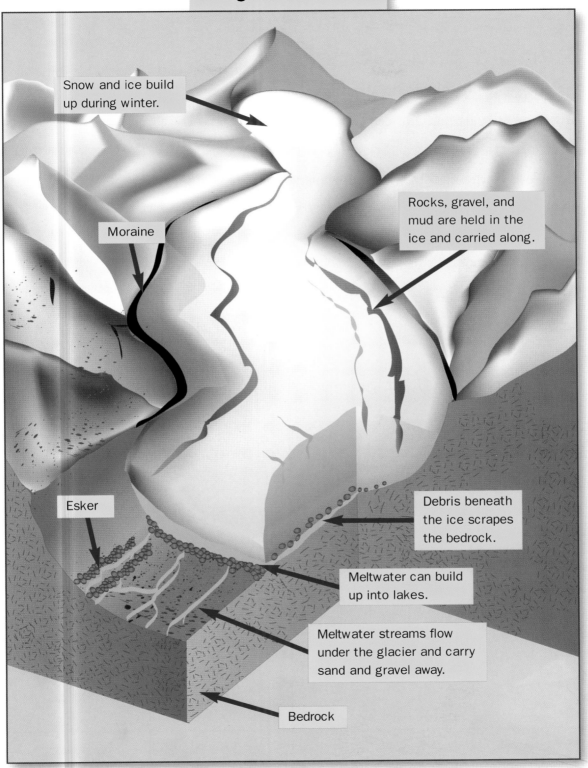

Snow and ice build up during winter.

Moraine

Rocks, gravel, and mud are held in the ice and carried along.

Esker

Debris beneath the ice scrapes the bedrock.

Meltwater can build up into lakes.

Meltwater streams flow under the glacier and carry sand and gravel away.

Bedrock

People and Glaciers

Scientists called glaciologists study glaciers for a number of reasons. One reason is to learn about their **effects** on Earth's surface. Another reason is to be aware of the effects they can have on people who live near them.

effects
changes caused by the action of forces

Changes in Earth's climate are causing changes in glaciers. Glaciers grow and shrink in response to changing temperature. If the temperature gets warmer, then glaciers will melt and retreat. If it gets colder, then glaciers will get bigger. The changes in glaciers usually happen very slowly. But any change can affect people's lives.

Glaciologists study how ice sheets are changing in Antarctica.

Global Warming Global warming, or the rising temperature of Earth's climate, is causing glaciers around the world to begin to melt or retreat. The Bering Glacier in North America has lost nearly 11.2 kilometers (7 miles) of its length in recent years.

Melting glaciers release large amounts of water and can cause very dangerous flooding. In the Himalaya, a large mountain range in Asia, there are dozens of mountain lakes that are full of water from melting glaciers. They are so full that they may overflow and cause floods. The lives of thousands of people who live in the mountains and in downstream villages are in danger.

This glacier is flowing into a lake in the Asian country of Kazakstan.

Water Shortages Melting glaciers caused by global warming can also lead to water shortages in other places. In several countries in South America and Asia, people rely on glaciers to supply water for drinking and agriculture. As glaciers get smaller and disappear, these people will have major water shortages.

Scientists and other experts from many countries often meet to discuss the problems caused by melting glaciers. They try to find ways to reduce the risks of flooding and water shortages, and to prevent disasters.

People in Pakistan dig a channel so glacier meltwater can flow to their fields and orchards.

Think About the Key Concepts

Think about what you read. Think about the pictures and the diagram. Use these to answer the questions. Share what you think with others.

1. Explain two ways that forces change Earth's surface.

2. Explain the difference between weathering and erosion.

3. In what ways can people be affected by the forces that shape Earth's surface?

4. In what ways can people control the effects of forces that shape Earth's surface?

Cutaway Diagram

Diagrams are pictures that show information.
You can learn new ideas without having to read many words. Diagrams use pictures and words to explain ideas.

There are different kinds of diagrams.
This diagram of how ice breaks rock is a **cutaway diagram**. A cutaway diagram is a three-dimensional picture that shows a "slice" of something, such as a slice of Earth. Look back at the diagram on page 13. It is a cutaway diagram of a glacier.

How to Read a Diagram

1. Read the title.
The title tells you what the diagram is about.

2. Read the labels.
Labels point out the important parts of the diagram.

3. Study the diagram.
Which parts of the diagram are on the surface, and which parts are beneath the surface?

4. Think about what you learned.
What did the cutaway diagram show you?

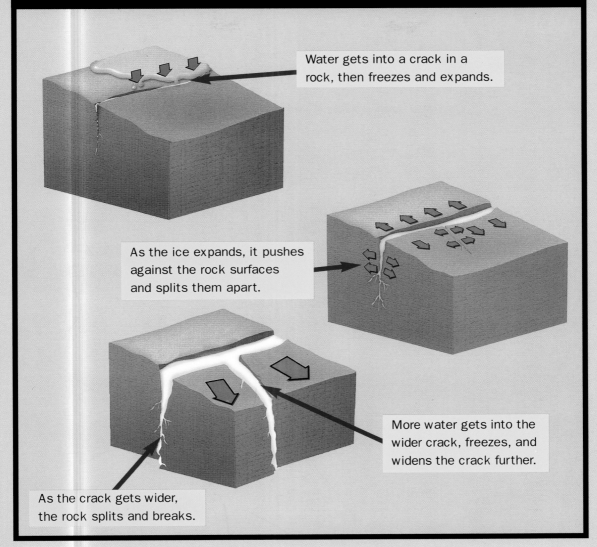

Water gets into a crack in a rock, then freezes and expands.

As the ice expands, it pushes against the rock surfaces and splits them apart.

More water gets into the wider crack, freezes, and widens the crack further.

As the crack gets wider, the rock splits and breaks.

What Did You Learn?

Read the diagram by following the steps on page 18. Write a short paragraph explaining what you learned. Then exchange paragraphs with a classmate. See if your paragraphs are clear to each other.

Cause and Effect Article

Cause and effect articles may describe an event. They tell why the event happened (the causes) and the results of the event (the effects). The article starting on page 21 describes the Ice Age.

Cause and effect articles generally include the following:

The Introduction
The introduction gives general details about the event that will be described in the article.

The Body Paragraphs
The first few body paragraphs explain the causes and the next paragraphs describe the effects.

The Conclusion
The conclusion explains how the event ended or describes possible future effects.

The Ice Age

The **title** tells what the article will be about.

There have been many ice ages, or periods in Earth's history when vast glaciers covered land. The last ice age began about 115,000 years ago and ended about 10,000 years ago. During this time, massive ice sheets covered most of North America and large regions in Europe and Asia.

The **introduction** gives general details about the event.

The Ice Age altered North America's landscape in numerous ways. Large glaciers carved out valleys by wearing away rock. In Utah, many canyons were created by the moving glaciers. In Wisconsin, a forest was crushed by the force of the moving ice. The glaciers also changed the landscape by carrying and depositing soils and rocks in different places.

Maps, **photographs**, or diagrams may support the text.

Glaciers like this one cover large areas of land during an ice age.

How the Ice Age Caused Changes

The Ice Age brought about many changes to the North American landscape. There are several causes for these changes. The average temperature during the Ice Age was about 8° Celsius (14° Fahrenheit) colder than average temperatures today. The summers were shorter and the winters were longer and colder. Snow that fell in winter did not melt completely during the short summer. Over time, more snow fell and huge layers of ice built up on the land.

These huge ice sheets, or glaciers, changed the landscape. As the glaciers moved over the land, they acted like giant bulldozers, scraping and eroding the land. They plowed away soil and wore down rocks. They also deposited heaps of soil along their way.

The weight of the glacial ice sheet made Earth's surface sink. This caused depressions in the land. The movement of the glaciers carved these depressions into basins and hollows.

First **body paragraphs** explain the causes.

When glaciers melt, vast plains and many different types of lakes and valleys are left behind. As the weight of the glaciers is removed, the sunken land below them begins to slowly move back up, changing the elevation, or height, of the landforms.

Glacial movement during the Ice Age carved these cliffs in Alaska.

Effects of the Ice Age

The Ice Age had a significant effect on the sea level around the world. This is because a large amount of water became "locked up" in glaciers as ice. Water from the sea evaporated and fell on glaciers as snow. Because the snow did not melt and flow back to the sea during the Ice Age, the sea level fell. About 21,000 years ago, the level of the sea was approximately 120 meters (390 feet) lower than it is today. The low sea level exposed areas of land that are now under water.

Next **body paragraphs** describe the effects.

Changing Coastlines

Sea level changes during and after the Ice Age changed the shape of North America's coastline. As the sea level got lower, more land was uncovered. For example, a land bridge between Asia and North America was uncovered in the Ice Age. This land bridge allowed people and animals to move from Asia to North America. When the Ice Age ended, the sea level rose and submerged the land bridge.

The Bering Land Bridge

Arctic Ocean

Chukchi Sea

ASIA

NORTH AMERICA

Key

Present-day land

Land bridge

Ocean

Bering Sea

0 mi.   500

0 km   500

Pacific Ocean

N
W E
S

This map shows the land bridge that joined Asia and North America in the last ice age. The land bridge is now covered by ocean.

A Changing Landscape

North America's landscape changed significantly as a result of the Ice Age. The movements and actions of ice changed the shape of many landforms. In some places, rivers and lakes were carved or moved by the powerful force of the advancing or retreating glaciers.

The Finger Lakes in New York were formed by moving ice during the Ice Age. The lakes were once river valleys. Along the rivers, the glacier scooped out U-shaped troughs that now contain deep lakes.

Till

Rocks and other material that became trapped in glaciers got crushed and deposited in different places. The deposited rock and other material, called till, was ground up within the glacier as it moved, and deposited as the glacier melted away. Glacial till is rich in minerals and makes very fertile soil for farmland.

During the last ice age, the ice sheets scraped huge amounts of soil from central Canada and deposited it on the central plains of the United States. The till made the central plains very fertile.

New York's Finger Lakes, as seen from space

Moraines

Large deposits of till created by melting glaciers made landforms called moraines. Moraines often show where a glacier used to be. Long Island and Cape Cod are examples of giant moraines left behind by the immense ice sheet of the last ice age.

Drumlins

Drumlins are another type of landform left behind by glaciers. The pointed ends of these long, teardrop-shaped formations show the direction the glacier was retreating.

Kettle Lakes

Kettle lakes are another landform caused by the Ice Age. Kettle lakes were made when chunks of ice broke off a retreating glacier and were left behind in the glacial gravel. Melted water from the glacier often carried sand and mud, which partly buried the block of ice. Over a long time, the ice melted and filled the cavity, creating a small lake.

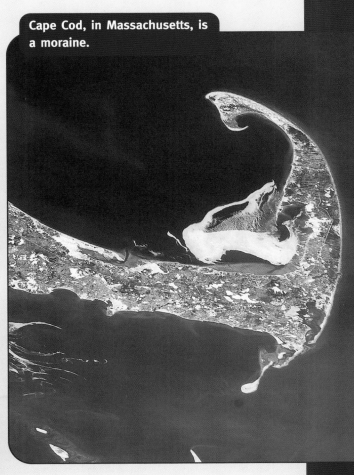

Cape Cod, in Massachusetts, is a moraine.

Drumlins in Manitoba, Canada

Kettle lakes in Northwest Territory, Canada

When the Ice Age Ended

The Ice Age ended about 10,000 years ago when Earth began to warm up again. The ice sheets melted and the sea level rose.

However, the effects of the Ice Age have lasted for a long time after the ice melted away. With the formation of numerous moraines, valleys, and lakes, North America's landscape permanently changed after the Ice Age.

The **conclusion** describes the end of the event or the future effects.

The Ice Age left behind many clues of its existence. Till, moraines, and drumlins are evidence of huge glaciers. Scientists can study soil, rock, and sand to learn about the Ice Age and how it changed the landscape.

Scientists predict that ice ages will continue to change the shape of Earth's surface in the future.

This peak in Yosemite National Park, Sierra Nevada, was shaped by glacial activity in the last ice age.

Apply the Key Concepts

Key Concept 1 Different forces shape the landforms that make up Earth's surface.

Activity

Draw a landscape with different landforms that are found on Earth's surface. Label the different landforms in your drawing.

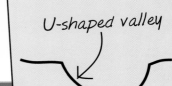

U-shaped valley

Key Concept 2 Earth's surface changes in different ways.

Activity

Choose an example of weathering and erosion caused by ice. Then draw a simple diagram to show the steps in the process.

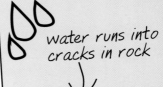

water runs into cracks in rock

Key Concept 3 People try to control, or at least understand, the effect of forces that shape Earth's surface.

Activity

Imagine you are a person affected by melting glaciers. Write a letter to a friend describing the changes brought about by the melting glacier and how it has affected you.

Dear Mary,

Write Your Own Cause and Effect Article

You have read the cause and effect article about an event in nature. Now you will write your own cause and effect article about an event you find interesting.

1. Study the Model

Look back at the description of cause and effect articles on page 20. Then read the introduction. What does it tell you about the topic? Read the body text. Think about how the information under the heading *How the Ice Age Caused Changes* is different from the information under the heading *Effects of the Ice Age*. Now read the conclusion, *When the Ice Age Ended*. Think about how the structure of this article helped you understand the topic.

Writing a Cause and Effect Article

◆ Choose an event with clear causes and effects.

◆ Write an introduction that gives general details about the event.

◆ Write "cause" paragraphs that tell why the event happened.

◆ Then write "effect" paragraphs that tell results of the event.

◆ Tell about the end of the event in your conclusion.

2. Choose Your Topic

Now choose an event in nature to write about. It should be an event that changed Earth's surface in some way, such as a landslide or an earthquake. You may find some ideas on the Internet or in books. Be sure to choose an event for which there are clear causes and effects.

3. Research Your Topic

Now that you have chosen your topic, you need to find more information about it. Use several different resources to find the information you need. Take notes as you come across important facts. Organize your information according to whether it is a cause or an effect.

Landslide

Cause: heavy rain

Cause: erosion

Effect: buildings destroyed

Effect: people killed

4. Write a Draft

Now it is time to write a draft of your article. First write the introduction. Give general information about the event, such as when and where it happened, how severe it was, and if people were affected. Write a section on the causes of the event and a section on the effects of the event. Finally, write a conclusion that explains how the event ended or describes possible future effects of the event.

5. Revise Your Draft

Read over what you have written. How clearly have you presented the information? Rewrite any unclear parts. Check against your research that all the facts you have included are accurate. Correct any spelling or punctuation errors that you find.

Create a Cause and Effect Chart

Follow the steps below to turn your article into a cause and effect chart. Then you can share your work with your classmates.

How to Make a Chart

1. Think of a heading.
Your heading should tell what the chart is about. Write the heading at the top of a large piece of paper.

2. Write down the causes.
Write the causes of the event in a list on the left-hand side of the piece of paper. You will not have much room for detail, so you will have to write brief notes. Draw a box around the list.

3. Write down the effects.
Write the effects in a list on the right-hand side of the piece of paper. Draw a box around the list.

4. Draw an arrow.
Draw an arrow across the page, linking the "causes" box to the "effects" box.

5. Illustrate your chart.
Add any diagrams or illustrations to make the text easier to understand.

6. Display your charts.
As a class, pin your charts to the classroom wall. Then move around the room, reading each other's charts. Be prepared to answer any questions about your chart.

Glossary

abrasion – the process of rubbing or scraping

bedrock – solid rock that lies beneath loose rock and soil on Earth's surface

chemical weathering – weathering caused by chemicals dissolving rock

deposition – the dropping or putting down of worn-down rock or soil

effects – changes caused by the action of forces

erosion – the moving of worn-down rock and soil to another place

eskers – long, narrow landforms made up of sand and gravel that were moved by water under a glacier

forces – causes of movement and change

glacier – a large, thick, moving mass of ice

landforms – natural shapes on Earth's surface

mechanical weathering – weathering caused by something pushing against rock, causing it to break

moraines – long landforms at the edges of a glacier made up of material moved by melting ice

outwashes – wide, flat plains made of sand and gravel that were moved by meltwater flowing out of a glacier

weathering – the wearing away of rock over time

Index